Working

Contents	Page

written by Pam Holden

Elephants use their trunks to help do their work.

elephant

They can lift big logs and carry heavy things.

3

Dogs can run fast to work for farmers.

sheep dogs

They can bark at sheep and cows to make them run.

5

Donkeys can carry heavy things on their backs.

They can take people for rides, too.

donkey

Pigeons can carry
messages for people.

8

They fly a long way with letters on their legs.

horse

Horses can run fast with people on their backs.

They can work pulling
heavy things, too.

Monkeys can climb up trees and pick coconuts.

monkey

They climb fast to the top to get the coconuts.

13

Camels can take people over the hot deserts. They can carry heavy things, too.

Camels don't have to stop to have a drink.

camels

Animals can help people do their work.